Fantastic
TUNES
for you to play

Compiled and arranged by Nick Freeth

Bath New York Singapore Hong Kong Cologne Delhi Melbourne

First published by Parragon in 2010

Parragon
Queen Street House
4 Queen Street
Bath BA1 1HE, UK

Designed, produced and packaged by
Stonecastle Graphics Limited

Compiled and arranged by Nick Freeth

ISBN 978-1-4075-4992-7

Printed in China

Contents

Introduction

This album contains a wide selection of guitar music, dating from the 16th century to recent times. It's in a range of idioms: there are classical compositions and transcriptions of lute and cittern pieces; arrangements of well-known folk songs and spirituals; and other works that may be less familiar, but will prove just as enjoyable to learn and perform. Most of them can be played with a pick, but those requiring the use of the right hand fingers are clearly identified.

The music is presented in standard notation as well as tablature: the latter provides valuable information about the location of notes on the fingerboard, but is far less flexible and detailed than the conventional five-line stave and its associated symbols.

Guitar music features two special kinds of notational symbol. A Roman numeral above the stave specifies the required **position** for the left hand on the fingerboard. When **II** is shown, your LH index finger should be ready to hold down notes at the second fret, while your middle, ring and little fingers are available to 'cover' the frets immediately above; when **III** is indicated, your index finger is placed on the third fret...and so on. A Roman numeral preceded by a **C** indicates that several notes are to be held down by a barré at a particular fret.

Where there's no Roman numeral, notes and chords can mostly be found at the guitar's 'open' position, though stretches onto higher frets may also be necessary.

As you familiarize yourself with the notation and tablature, you may find it helpful to study them in conjunction with the recordings of the pieces supplied on the accompanying CD. However, the disc is only intended as a guide: you should strive to develop your own interpretation of each item, and practise slowly and persistently. Before long, your efforts will be rewarded by the satisfaction of being able to play this wonderful music for yourself.

Introduction to the Guitar: Study 5

Fernando Sor (1778–1839) Op.60

Play steadily and evenly: use a pick or fingers

Introduction to the Guitar: Study 5

Two Waltzes

From *Companion for the Guitar* by Robert Kelley (1855)

I. Havana Waltz. Play smoothly, with a pick or fingerstyle

Two Waltzes

II. Copenhagen Waltz. Play fingerstyle, with a well-marked rhythm

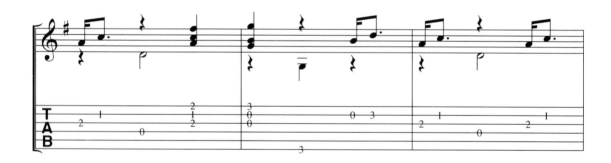

Two Waltzes

Introduction to the Guitar: Study 6

Fernando Sor (1778–1839) Op.60

To be played fingerstyle (not with a pick), and fairly fast

Introduction to the Guitar: Study 6

Introduction to the Guitar: Study 6

John, Come Kiss Me Now

British traditional tune; this version is freely adapted from cittern tablature
in a Scottish Commonplace Book by Robert Edwards (c.1650)

Simple Gifts

Words and music by Shaker Elder Joseph Brackett Jr. (1797–1882)

Not too slow

Simple Gifts

love   and   de - light. _____

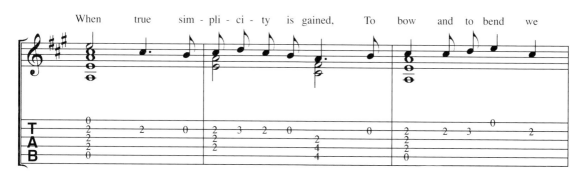

When   true   sim - pli - ci - ty   is gained,   To   bow   and   to bend   we

shan't   be   a - shamed,   To   turn,   turn   will   be   our   de - light,   'Til by

turn - ing,   turn - ing we   come round   right. ___

Tant Que Vivray

Melody by Claudin de Sermisy (c.1490–1562)

At a moderate speed. Play fingerstyle.

Tant Que Vivray

Tant Que Vivray

Greensleeves

Traditional English

Fairly slow; flexible speed

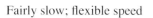

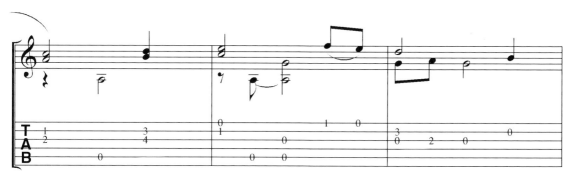

Greensleeves

Greensleeves

Greensleeves

Greensleeves

Coventry Carol

Adapted from the Pageant of the Shearmen and Tailors (1591)

Quite slow; play fingerstyle

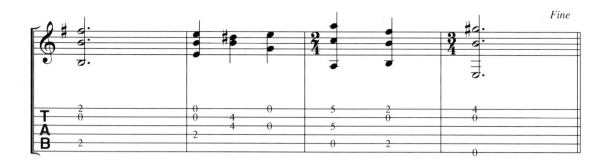

Fine

Coventry Carol

D.C. al Fine

Go Down, Moses

Traditional spiritual

Fairly slow

Go Down, Moses

Go Down, Moses

Go Down, Moses

Minuet (1686)

Robert de Visée (c.1650–c.1725)

Poised and stately; play fingerstyle

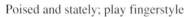

Minuet (1686)

Sloop John B

Traditional West Indian song – relaxed tempo

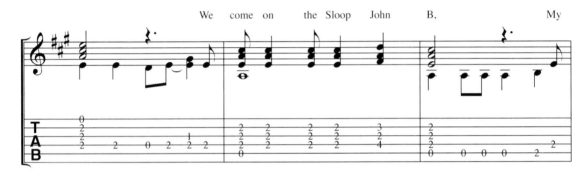

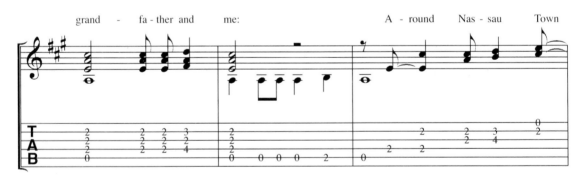

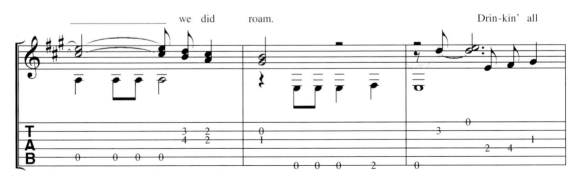

Sloop John B

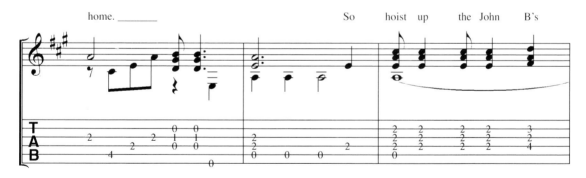

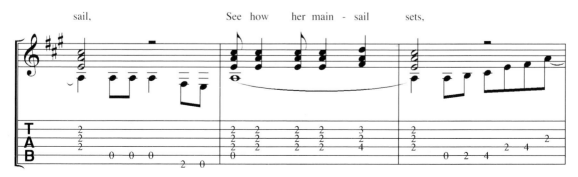

Sloop John B

Sloop John B

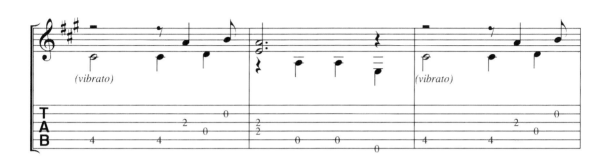

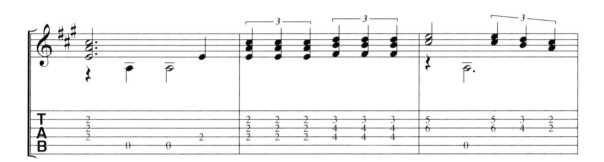

Let me go home, _____

Let me go home, _____ I

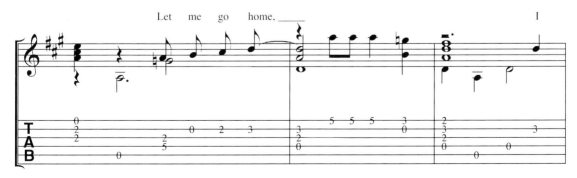

Sloop John B

What Shall We Do With the Drunken Sailor?

Traditional sea shanty

With a driving rhythm

What shall we do with the drun-ken sai-lor,

what shall we do with the drun-ken sai-lor,

What Shall We Do With the Drunken Sailor?

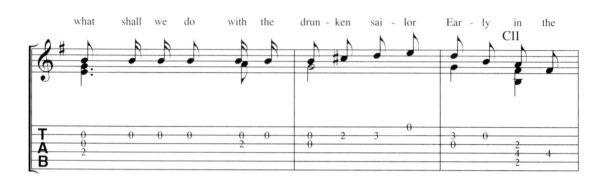

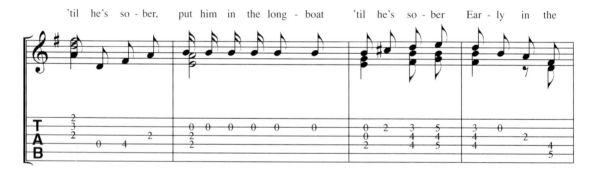

What Shall We Do With the Drunken Sailor?

What Shall We Do With the Drunken Sailor?

Hoo - ray, and up she ri - ses, hoo - ray, and up she ri - ses,

hoo - ray, and up she ri - ses, Ear - ly in the morn - ing.

We Wish You a Merry Christmas

Traditional English

On chords marked ✳, mute the 5th string with the finger fretting the 6th string

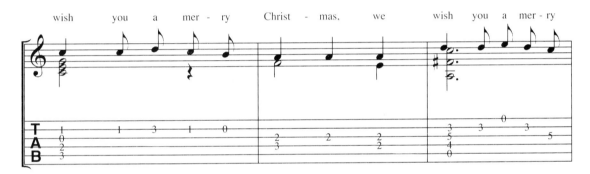

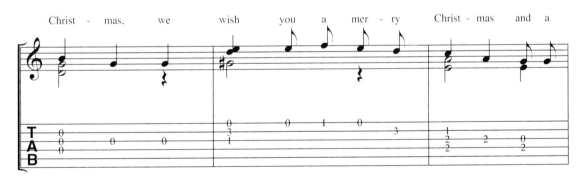

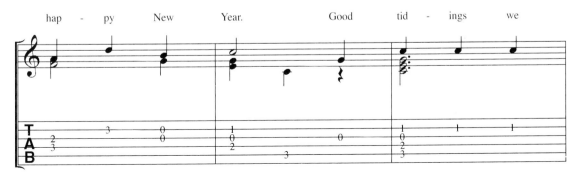

We Wish You a Merry Christmas

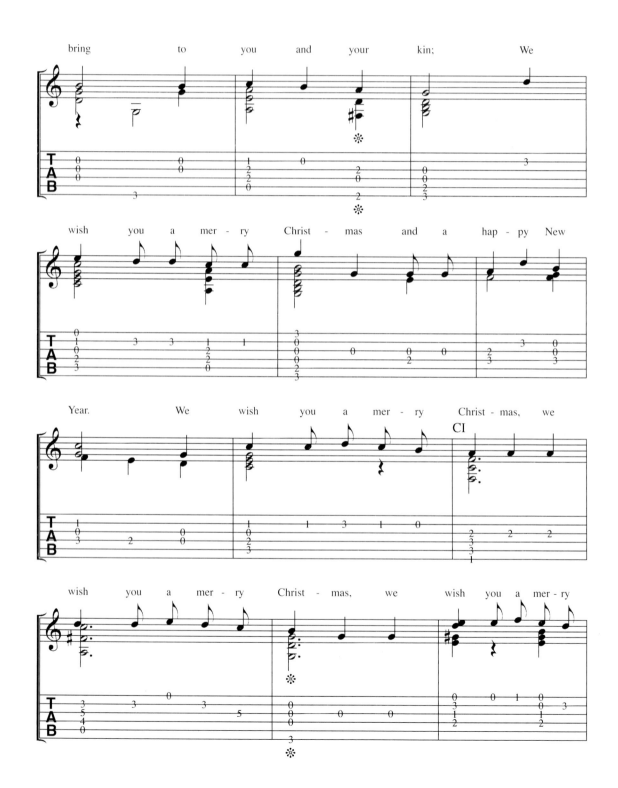

We Wish You a Merry Christmas

Pavane

Luis Milan (1536–1561)

Slowly and majestically; play fingerstyle (not with a pick)

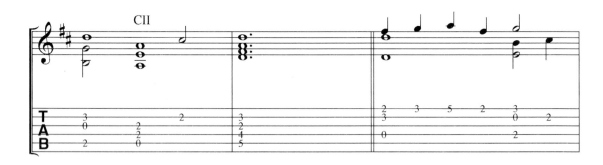

Pavane

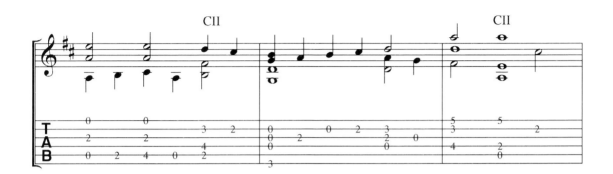

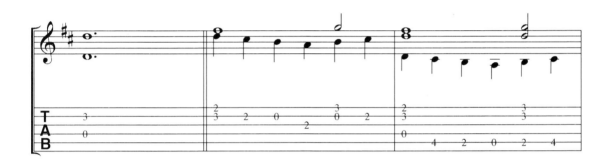

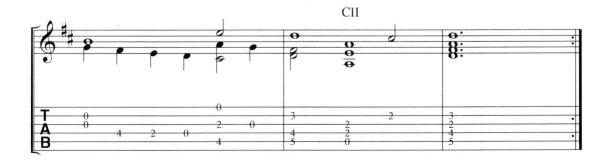

Two Irish Jigs

Traditional

Play these classic dance tunes fluently and fairly fast
I. The Blarney Pilgrim

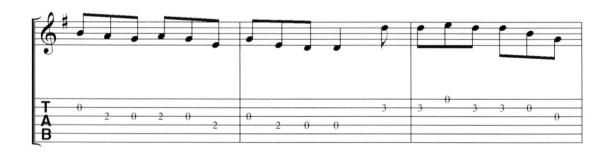

Two Irish Jigs

48

Two Irish Jigs

II. The Irish Washerwoman

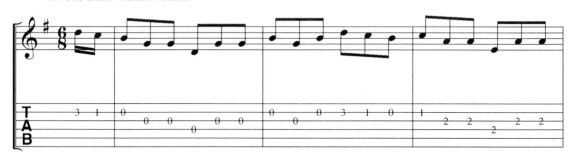

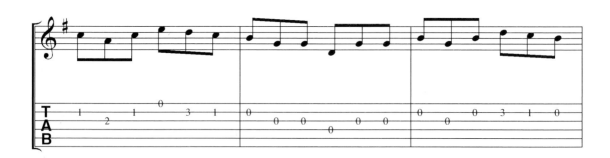

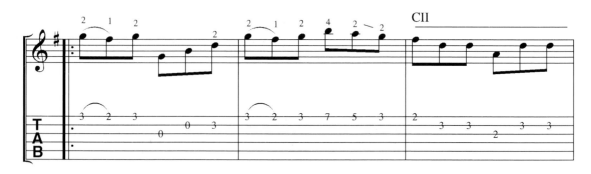

Two Irish Jigs

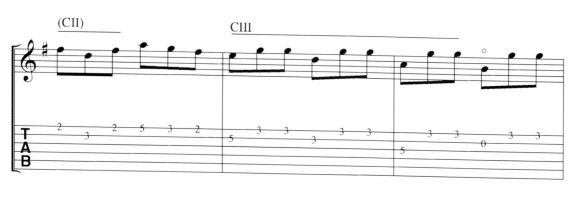

Nobody Knows the Trouble I've Seen

Traditional spiritual

Nobody Knows the Trouble I've Seen

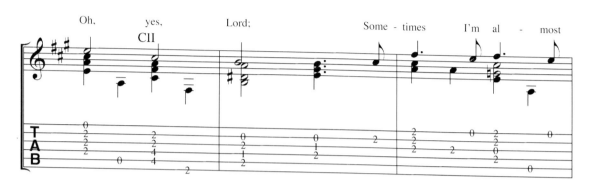

Nobody Knows the Trouble I've Seen

Nobody Knows the Trouble I've Seen

St. Anne's Reel

Traditional French-Canadian

St. Anne's Reel

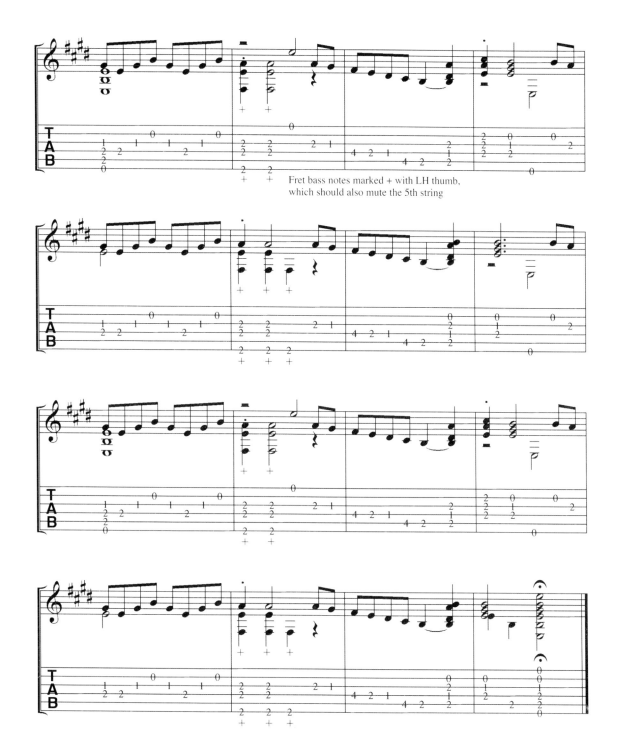

Fret bass notes marked + with LH thumb,
which should also mute the 5th string

Ding Dong, Merrily on High

Branle de l'Officiel (Servant's Dance) from *Orchésographie* by Thoinot Arbeau (1519–1595)

Ding Dong, Merrily on High

Whiskey in the Jar

Traditional Irish

Wherever there's a horizontal line above the stave, play all the upper notes on
the 2nd string, sliding up and down with your left-hand fingers as necessary.

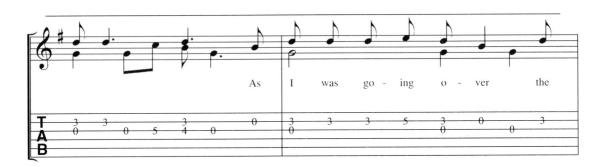

As   I   was   go - ing   o - ver   the

far - fam'd Ker - ry   moun - tains,   I   met with Colo - nel Far - rell and his

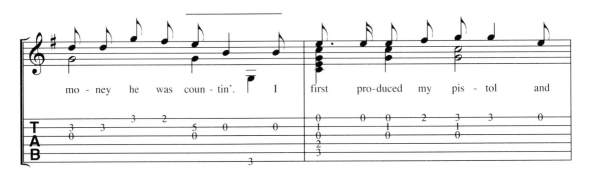

mo - ney   he   was   coun - tin'.   I   first   pro - duced   my   pis - tol   and

Whiskey in the Jar

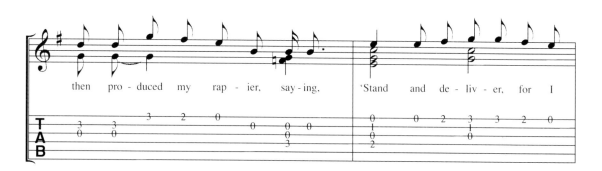

then pro - duced my rap - ier, say - ing, 'Stand and de - liv - er, for I

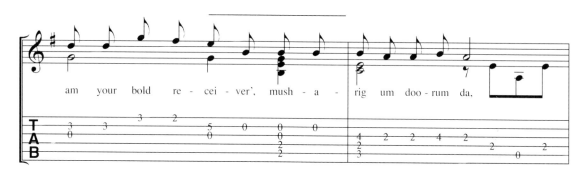

am your bold re - cei - ver', mush - a - rig um doo - rum da,

Whack fol the dad - dy - o, Whack fol the dad - dy - o, there's

whis - key in the jar.

Whiskey in the Jar

Whiskey in the Jar

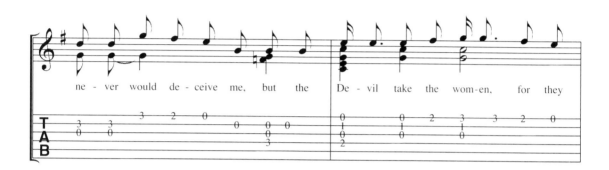

ne - ver would de - ceive me, but the De - vil take the wom - en, for they

al - ways lie so ea - sy, mush - a - rig um doo - rum da,

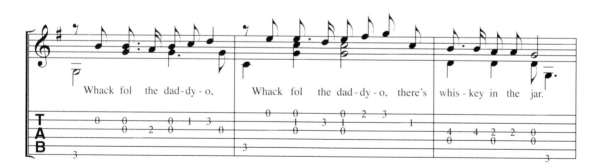

Whack fol the dad - dy - o, Whack fol the dad - dy - o, there's whis - key in the jar.

House of the Rising Sun

Traditional American

Slowly; sustain notes by keeping them held down, and allowing open strings to ring

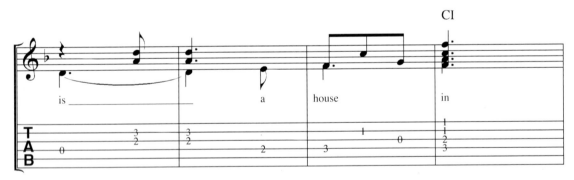

House of the Rising Sun

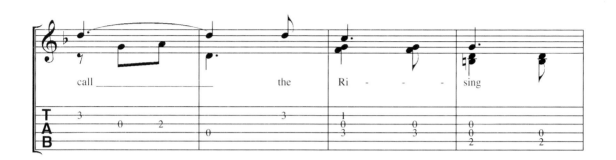

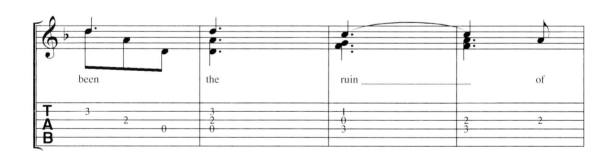

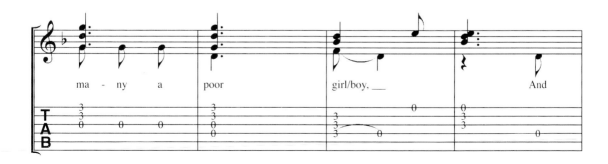

House of the Rising Sun

House of the Rising Sun

House of the Rising Sun

En Filant Ma Quenouille

French-Canadian tune from *Chansons Populaires du Canada* (1894)

Vigorously.   On chords marked ❄, mute the 5th string with the finger fretting the 6th string

En Filant Ma Quenouille

En Filant Ma Quenouille

All Through the Night

Traditional Welsh melody; words adapted from Sir Harold Boulton (1859–1935)

Allow the harmonics (marked ◇) to ring

All Through the Night

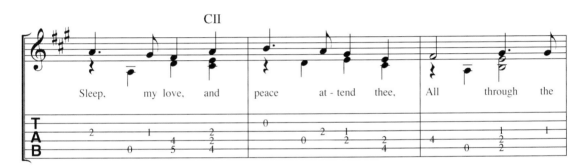

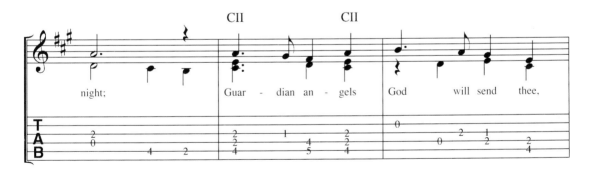

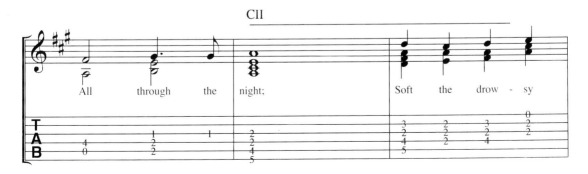

All Through the Night

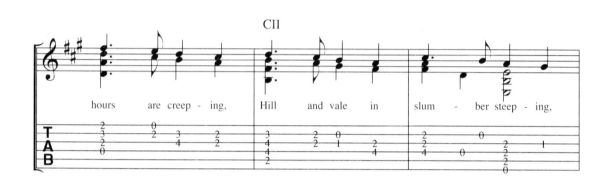

hours   are creep - ing,   Hill   and vale   in   slum - ber steep - ing,

I   my lov - ing   vi - gil keep - ing,   All   through   the

night. _____   (Slower and softer)

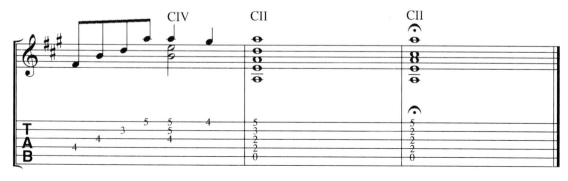

Oh, Susanna

Stephen Foster (1826–1864)

Oh, Susanna

rained   all   night   the   day   I   left,   the   wea - ther   it   was

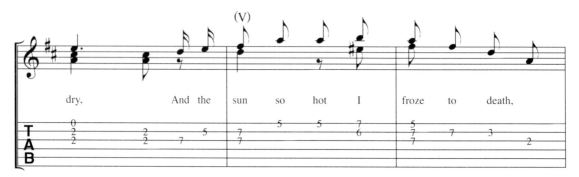

dry,   And   the   sun   so   hot   I   froze   to   death,

Su - san - na,   don't   you   cry.

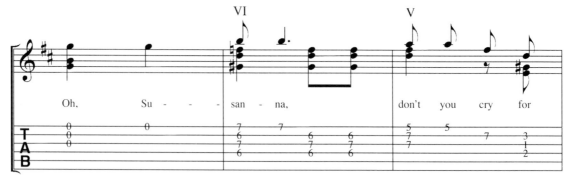

Oh,   Su -   - san - na,   don't   you   cry   for

Oh, Susanna

Molly Malone

Molly Malone

Tarleton's Resurrection

John Dowland (1563–1626)

Slow and dignified; play fingerstyle

Tarleton's Resurrection

Two Tunes From 'The Dancing Master'

John Playford (1st edition, 1651) I. Half Hannikin – play fingerstyle, at a lively tempo

Two Tunes From 'The Dancing Master'

Two Tunes From 'The Dancing Master'

II. Newcastle – play fingerstyle, at a moderate speed

Two Tunes From 'The Dancing Master'

Three Swedish 'Polskas'

Tunes from *Traditioner af Swenska Folk-Dansar*, Part 1 (1814)

Polska I – vigorously: play fingerstyle. Slide LH fingers where ～ is shown

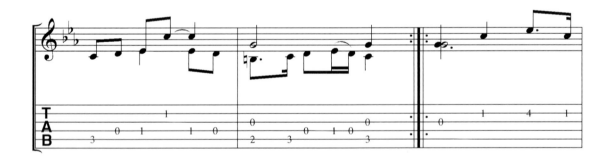

Three Swedish 'Polskas'

Polska II. Slower and more gently: play fingerstyle

Three Swedish 'Polskas'

Three Swedish 'Polskas'

Polska III. A little faster: play fingerstyle

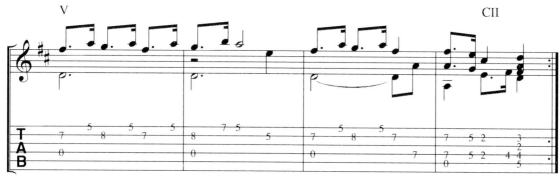

Three Scottish Folk Melodies

Traditional

I. The Campbells Are Coming: moderate speed

Three Scottish Folk Melodies

Three Scottish Folk Melodies

Three Scottish Folk Melodies

III. Auld Lang Syne

Three Scottish Folk Melodies